D1059691

LEVEL **2** SCIENCE

LET'S READ AND FIND OUT

HOW TO TALK TO YOUR COMPUTER

BY SEYMOUR SIMON · ILLUSTRATED BY MIKE LOWERY

HARPER

An Imprint of HarperCollinsPublishers

Special thanks to Dr. Justin Solomon, Assistant Professor at Massachusetts Institute of Technology, and to Joey Jachowski, for their valuable assistance.

The Let's-Read-and-Find-Out Science book series was originated by Dr. Franklyn M. Branley, Astronomer Emeritus and former Chairman of the American Museum of Natural History—Hayden Planetarium, and was formerly co-edited by him and Dr. Roma Gans, Professor Emeritus of Childhood Education, Teachers College, Columbia University. Text and illustrations for each of the books in the series are checked for accuracy by an expert in the relevant field. For more information about Let's-Read-and-Find-Out Science books, write to HarperCollins Children's Books, 195 Broadway, New York, NY 10007, or visit our website at www.letsreadandfindout.com.

Let's Read-and-Find-Out Science® is a trademark of HarperCollins Publishers.

How to Talk to Your Computer
Text copyright © 1985, 2019 by Seymour Simon
Illustrations by Mike Lowery
Illustrations copyright © 2019 by HarperCollins Publishers
All rights reserved. Manufactured in China.
No part of this book may be used or reproduced in any manner whatsoever without written permission except in the case of brief quotations embodied in critical articles and reviews. For information address HarperCollins Children's Books, a division of HarperCollins Publishers, 195 Broadway, New York, NY 10007.
www.harpercollinschildrens.com

Library of Congress Control Number: 2018952016
ISBN 978-0-06-249087-2 (trade bdg.) — ISBN 978-0-06-249086-5 (pbk.)

The artist used pen and ink and digital media to create the digital illustrations for this book.
Typography by Erica De Chavez
18 19 20 21 22 SCP 10 9 8 7 6 5 4 3 2 1
❖
New Edition, 2019

For my son, Robert, my
favorite computer scientist
—S.S.

To my favorite people,
Katrin, Allister, and Okar
—M.L.

"Please throw me the ball," you tell your friend.

Your friend picks up the ball and throws it to you. But he could have done a number of things, such as bounce the ball or throw it to another person.

If you tell your **computer** to throw you the ball, the computer will always do the same thing. The computer is totally obedient and does exactly what you want. The challenge is speaking a language the computer can understand.

You must tell a computer exactly what you want it to do, step-by-step. If you leave out a step, the computer will do things wrong. Or it will just not know what to do. Unlike your friend, the computer doesn't know how to do much without your help!

All robots are run by computers. You can think of the computer as the robot's brain.

Imagine that you have a robot friend. You call it EZ.

EZ stands still. "Beep, beep, error," it says. It doesn't know how to do what you ask. It needs more complete directions.

12

"This is what I want you to do," you tell EZ.

① Pick up the ball with your right hand.

② Bring your right hand back over your head.

③ Move your right hand forward quickly toward me and release the ball.

Now the computer in the robot can follow your directions. EZ picks up the ball and . . .

14

Your friend can do the same things that you told EZ the robot to do. But he does not have to be told how to do it step-by-step. He knows what you mean because he has thrown a ball many times in the past.

A digital tablet and a smartphone are computers, too. They can't do new things unless you give them exact instructions. If you want a computer to do something new, you have to tell it what to do.

17

We tell a computer what to do by using a computer program. A **program** is a list of steps to follow to do a task, like throwing a ball. These steps are called **statements** when you write them for computers. You also have to write programs in **programming languages** that computers can understand.

Programs can be short or long. Some computer programs are thousands of steps long. Others are only two or three steps long.

Here is a short program for you. Make believe *you* are a computer. Read all three steps in this program and then follow them.

KID COMPUTERS

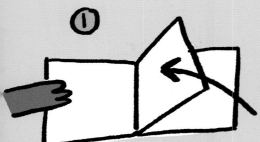

① Turn over this page.

② Look at the top of the left-hand page.

③ Read the red letters.

CONGRATULATIONS!

You followed the steps in the program correctly.

How do you tell a computer the program you want it to follow? One way is to use a **keyboard** to talk to a computer. You type letters, numbers, and symbols such as * and **?** on the keyboard.

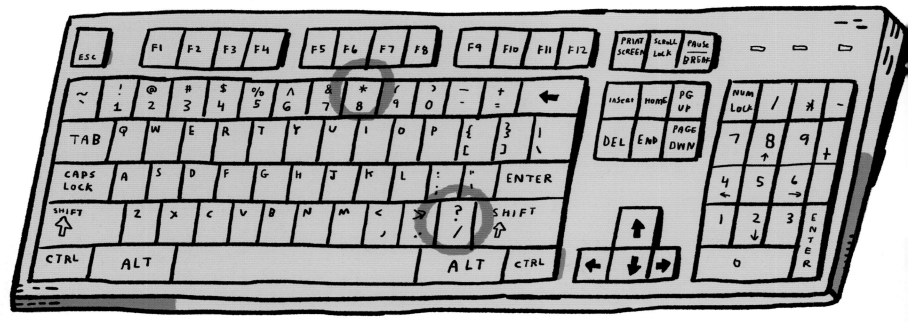

The letters, numbers, and symbols you type on the keyboard tell the computer what to do.

You can talk to some computers or they can talk to you, too. A computer talks to you with pictures or words on a screen called a **monitor**. It can also talk out loud with words from **speakers**.

Tablets and smartphones have speakers, screens, and keyboards, too.

How do programs work exactly? Think back to when you told EZ to throw the ball. There are only three steps in the program for throwing a ball, so it's important EZ does them in the right order. If EZ tried to throw the ball before it picked it up, EZ would just get confused.

In all programs, big and small, you need to make sure the steps happen in the right order.

If EZ was building a house, for example, what if it started with the roof before the walls? That wouldn't really work.

When you talk to computers, you have to make sure you tell them exactly what to do and *when* you want them to do it. Otherwise, they might get things wrong. . . .

Now, what if you told EZ how to jump rope? You and your friend would each hold one end of the rope and then start moving it in circles over EZ's head, but EZ might not know what to do. Even if you told EZ to jump, it might do it too early or too late.

EZ should jump only if the rope is about to come around and swing under its feet. This kind of "if-then" is called a **conditional** statement.

DON'T JUMP IF THE ROPE IS IN THE AIR.

JUMP IF THE ROPE IS ON THE GROUND.

If the rope is about to hit the ground in front of you, *then* jump! Look at that! EZ learned how to jump over the rope.

A LOOP

At the moment, EZ jumps only one time. If you want EZ to keep jumping over the rope, you have to tell it what to do every time! Instead of repeating yourself, let's change our instructions at the beginning to tell EZ to jump over the rope 10 times.

Now EZ will do the action 10 times and you don't need to repeat yourself! In a program, this way of repeating an action is called a **loop**.

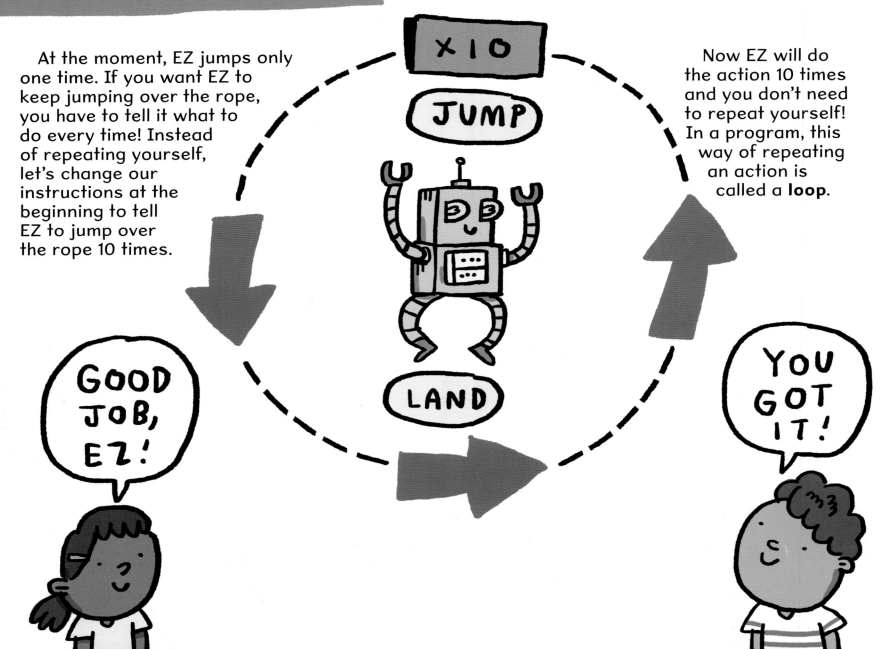

X 10

JUMP

LAND

GOOD JOB, EZ!

YOU GOT IT!

Loops tell the computer to do something a certain number of times. It could be one time or a thousand. Say you wanted to teach EZ how to use a yo-yo.

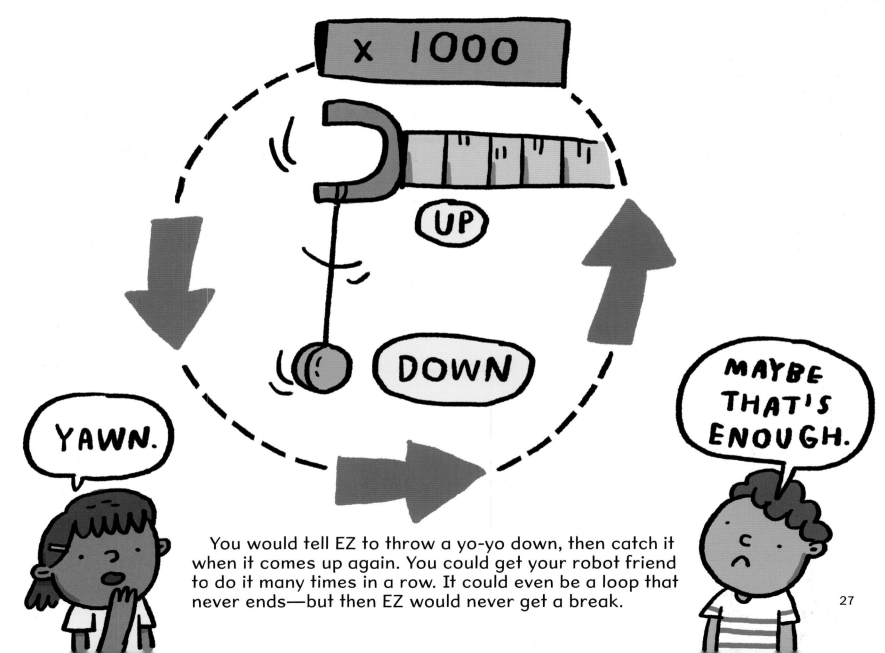

You would tell EZ to throw a yo-yo down, then catch it when it comes up again. You could get your robot friend to do it many times in a row. It could even be a loop that never ends—but then EZ would never get a break.

A FUNCTION

Now you know how to tell EZ all kinds of instructions! But wouldn't it be easier if you didn't need to say the instructions every single time? Otherwise, programming would probably be a real pain.

When you write a program, you write down the instructions in something called a **function**. It's like a recipe your computer can look at when you tell it what to do. For example, you could give EZ the recipe for making a peanut butter sandwich.

PEANUT BUTTER SANDWICH

① Take two slices of bread, a jar of peanut butter, and a butter knife.

② Lay the slices of bread side by side.

③ Use the knife to spread peanut butter on one slice.

④ Pick up the other slice and place it on the first slice.

You can have functions for everything you want EZ to do. After you give EZ the functions it should know, then your program is as simple as "Hi, EZ, today we're going to first make a *peanut butter sandwich*, then *jump rope*, and finally *play catch*."

MAKE A PEANUT BUTTER SANDWICH

JUMP ROPE

PLAY CATCH

Functions make programs easier to write and understand. And it means that you only need to get the instructions right the first time. When you combine functions, conditionals, and loops, you can really start to make your computer do amazing things!

HERE'S WHAT WE'VE LEARNED!

Now you know how to talk to your computer. You can talk to your computer by giving instructions on a keyboard. The instructions must be step-by-step, and they have to be in order. Computer instructions are called a program and they use things like statements, conditionals, and functions to tell computers what to do.

Learning to talk to your computer is like learning a new language. At first it doesn't make sense, and you're not even sure what you want to say.

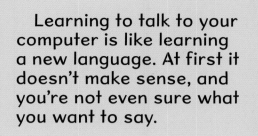

But after you learn how to talk to your computer, you'll find lots of things you want to tell it to do.

A ROBOT GAME

LEAD YOUR ROBOT FRIEND TO THE BURIED TREASURE BY WRITING A COMPUTER PROGRAM!

What you need:

A friend

Construction paper & safety scissors

A pen or pencil

A small player token like a penny or paper clip

Instructions:

1. On a piece of paper, draw a tic-tac-toe board.
2. Cut out 9 squares of construction paper. The squares need to be able to fit into the tic-tac-toe spaces.
3. On one of those squares, draw a treasure chest. (Construction paper helps so you can't see which square has the treasure from the other side.)
4. Turn the treasure chest square over. Arrange the papers so each piece is on a section of the tic-tac-toe board. Your friend can't see which square contains the treasure chest.
5. It's time to write your computer program on a separate piece of paper! Use arrow symbols to lead your robotic friend to the treasure. Keep in mind: your friend starts in the bottom left corner.

So, if you decide to put the treasure in the very top right corner, your instructions might look like this:

6. Next, give your friend the computer program. Your friend will be acting like a robot does when you give the robot a computer program. Your robot friend starts in the bottom left corner. Put an object there to mark where they start, like a penny or a paper clip.
7. Your robot friend should move their object across the pieces of paper, following the computer program you wrote to the treasure. Flip over the paper. Did you find it?

THIS SQUARE WOULD BE FLIPPED OVER!

This book aligns with the Next Generation Science Standards.
Find out more at nextgenscience.org.

This book meets the Common Core State Standards for Science
and Technical Subjects. For Common Core resources for this title
and others, please visit www.readcommoncore.com.

Online Resources and Getting Started

Today, anyone who has a computer and internet access has the ability to start programming! There are countless free online resources to use, many of which are targeted at helping you learn the basics of programming. Often, these programs use drag-and-drop languages that involve clicking blocks together on the screen to make things happen.

Here is a small sample of the resources available:

Hour of Code (hourofcode.com) is a series of one-hour lessons that teach the basics of coding and computer learning. In the last few years, more than 100 million kids and adults have tried the Hour of Code. It's an easy and fun way to learn how to talk to your computer.

Code.org (code.org) If you loved the Hour of Code but want to learn more, code.org has game-like lessons for all ages—even kindergarten.

ScratchJr (www.scratchjr.org) is a programming language specially designed for youngsters. It's available to learn, use, and have fun with through a free app and was inspired by a popular programming language developed by the Massachusetts Institute of Technology.

GLOSSARY

Computer – a device that carries out actions, makes decisions, and stores information (a robot's brain)

Condition or a conditional – a statement that helps computers decide when and if to do something

Function – a set of instructions in a program that can be called and executed by a specific name

Keyboard – a device people use to input letters and symbols into a computer

Loop – part of a program that tells a computer to do something for a certain amount of time or number of times

Monitor – a device that displays images and pictures from a computer

Program – a set of instructions that computers use to carry out actions

Programming language – a specific set of words and rules that programs are structured around so that computers can understand them

Speakers – a device that outputs audio and sound from a computer

Statement – a step in a program; a line of code